Contents

Introduction.

During more than twenty years as a salesperson, a sales manager, a regional sales director, and then back on the sales floor, I have always seen the long and boring training documents and videos that corporations make their newly hired, and experienced, salespeople go through. Across all companies the sales training courses have one thing in common: they teach the salespeople step by step how to dress, how to behave, and what to say to be successful. Likewise, the salespeople who study those training documents and videos have one thing in common: they become traditional salespeople. I have gone through the sales training and I did find it long and boring. When I was thrown on the sales floor, I tried to apply what I learned but found that most of it was obsolete because the sales process is dynamic, not static and chronological as the training presented.

The vast majority of the salespeople across any retail industry stick to applying what they learned in the sales training. The result: high turnover, not realizing one's income potential, and low efficiency and effectiveness.

The very few like me who deviated from the sales training and developed and applied their own methods were called the top salespeople. The result: low turnover, high income, high efficiency on the sales floor, and great customer service.

However, I took my methods a step further. Over the years I became more and more unorthodox with the customers. Meaning I became less and less traditional in the way I dress, the way I talk to the customers, and the way I close my sales. Many will wonder how I got away with breaking the rules on the floor. The answer is simple: because of my performance I was granted many privileges. Year after year of being increasingly non-traditional, I noticed that the results were better each year and that my methods were unique and were not being applied by other salespeople. When I became a sales manager, I asked the new hires to go through the training just to be politically correct but my training using my methods dominated the formal sales training. Not until I realized firsthand that my non-traditional sales techniques could be easily applied across different salespeople's age groups and personality types that I decided to write a book. When I became a regional sales director for a big multinational company, I wrote this book but never published it. However, I always communicated my ideas when I had the chance.

So, this short practical guide outlines my non-traditional sales techniques in an unstructured and simple manner. It is for the benefit of salespeople and sales managers. After reading this guide the hope is that both salespeople and sales managers would start a gradual application of the sales techniques explained in it. When the expected results are realized then more and more salespeople and managers would use it thus affecting a gradual change in a company. I was in a position to implement such a change for my region and the results were salespeople who turned their jobs into careers and salespeople that achieved advanced commissions and salaries.

This guide is not about Point-of-Sale systems. It is not about warranty policies. It is not about product return policies or customer service. And it is not about a retailer's product quality or inventory availability. It is about the salespeople and the sales managers. It is about thinking outside the box to earn the customer's business TODAY in a world that is witnessing an ever-increasing competition including online shopping, and in a world where over the years the customers have gotten tired of the stereotypical salesperson who through the way he/she looks, behaves, and talks is "just being a salesperson".

This guide is applicable to any retail sales setting; It can be applied to both salaried and commissioned sales activities across any industry. Again as I have seen them, the results of this deviation from the traditional sales methods were more productivity, less staff attrition, advanced commissions and salaries, easier management of staff, and better corporate bottom lines.

Chapter One: Dress Down, Not Up.

For years the sales literature that managers have used for training has always emphasized dressing up for success. While it is a good idea to dress up for success, the manager and salesperson must be mindful of several factors. On the other hand, when we talk about the dress code we need to talk about the men and the women separately.

If the salesman is to dress up by wearing a suit and tie, then that suit and tie must fit properly and must look good on the individual. More often than not, suits and ties that the salesmen wear are either too small or too large because they come from an old wardrobe or a relative's wardrobe. The customers will notice, as they have been forever, that the salesman is wearing that suit because he has to not because he wants to. The customers will notice that the salesman's suit and tie do not fit properly. The customers will also know if that salesman wears the same suit and tie every day. Suits and ties are expensive and the corporation and/or the salesman will usually not invest in a good appearance. I have always found it strange that the company expects its salespeople to look good and presentable, but they almost never offer any benefits to its salespeople to buy proper dress up clothes.

How many times have you seen the late Steve Jobs or Bill Gates wear a suit and tie? Both of these individuals are salespersons. They both can afford very well fit and expensive suits and ties, but they usually opt for jeans and casual shirts even when they appear on TV.

Once a customer notices anything about the salesman's appearance as mentioned above, the chances of that salesman closing a sale diminish. Customers would like to deal with comfortable salesmen who look good and smell good. They are turned off by salesmen who pretend to look good or pretend to be comfortable. The appearance of salespeople will be a major factor in success. Appearance definitely paves the way to the formation of strong positive impressions. Any sales manager should care about the personal grooming habits of the salespeople on the salesforce. Proper appearance gives the impression of professionalism and contributes to trustworthiness and respect. Also, proper grooming instills confidence in salespeople. Grooming can impact the attractiveness of a person and it falls into three categories:

- **Cleanliness**: Things like hair, teeth, nails, breath, and personal hygiene. Customers notice all of these.
- **Wardrobe**. As outlined above.
- **Attitude**: The salesperson should present a positive and confident attitude complemented by a clean smile that elicits trust.

So, grooming, good appearance, and comfort do not mean wearing a suit and tie. Professionalism also does not mean wearing a suit and tie. The salesman can definitely be underdressed compared to the customer and can still achieve success with that customer.

We can easily conclude from above that managers can achieve a groomed professional salesman without the need to make that salesman wear a suit and tie. Managers should rather have comfortable salesmen than salesmen wearing suits and ties that do not fit or that make them look awkward to their customers.

When it comes to saleswomen, the same issues apply except a saleswoman does not have to wear long boots or high heels in order to look professional and groomed. Saleswomen should also be comfortable and should feel comfortable. Saleswomen usually have it easier than salesmen because they look good by nature and they are viewed as less of a threat to the customer than salesmen.

Getting more women into retail sales has become a hot topic over the years, as this field has historically had a low representation of females. As a result, several organizations have surfaced to help close the gender disparity gap in sales. Despite these great efforts, the US Department of Commerce still reports that only 24% of sales jobs are held by women. So, managers need to get more women into sales professions. This percentage has only increased by 3% over the past decade. Not surprisingly, the percentage decreases as seniority increases, with the lowest percentage of women represented in manager and VP positions. Only 21% of Vice Presidents in Sales are female.

There are a number of reasons why this might be the case. Women may have preconceived notions about what it means to be in a sales profession. Sales can have a negative connotation to women who still think of the stereotypical used car salesman hungry to do whatever it takes to close the deal. After reading this guide hopefully that connotation will change.

What is it like as a woman to work in sales that is dominated by men? What's it like to be a woman in sales? Many women feel like there is no career path in sales, but many women in sales have organized to debunk that myth. They opened up about their careers and challenges, and inspired others to consider exploring sales positions in many industries.

Dressing down for men and women also has other advantages. When a salesperson is dressed down, he or she can move around more easily thus offering better service levels; he or she would be better able to show the customer that they are more engaged and more receptive to answer all the customer's needs, thus increasing the chances to close the sale.

Managers should see the advantages of being a non-traditional salesperson when it comes to appearance. Customers know that when they walk in, they are expecting salespeople dressed up. It is time to surprise the customers by offering them a breath of fresh air. This includes managers as well. It is time for managers to also dress down. From my long experience when customers see a dressed down manager, they feel more comfortable talking to him or her, and are usually more relaxed and more accepting of the resolution offered to them so they would be less likely to escalate the matter further in case of an issue. On the other hand, a dressed down manager when used as a second face will be more effective in closing the sale. We will discuss the second face later.

Chapter Two: Greet The Customer, Or Not.

Each retail company has absolutely no shortage of material to offer its salespeople on how to greet the customer when they walk into a store or a showroom. I know companies teach the salespeople AND monitor them on how to greet the customer; what to say in their greeting, when to say it, and where to stand and how far to stand when they greet their customers. I also know that corporations truly believe that greeting the customers is one pillar of good customer service and it increases the chance of closing the sale. Let's look at one example: Apple Inc.

Although this example should be qualified, throughout the world if you walk into an Apple store you will not be greeted by anyone. The salespeople at the Apple store do not even try to talk to the customer unless and until the customer starts asking questions. We all thought that greeting is one pillar of good customer service, so how come Apple employees do not greet customers?

Yet if we look at Apple's customer satisfaction, we will see that they have excellent ratings consistently.

From decades of experience my advice to salespeople and managers is to smile at the customer and not say anything when they come in the store, or if something has to be said it should be two words: Good Day. Enough making comments about the weather, or complementing the customer's clothes, or discussing how cute the baby is, or making comments about one's own children.

Long ago greeting a customer with a friendly "How are you?" was welcomed and returned with genuine customer interest. These days it is not the case. Instead, customers want to be approached in a friendly way that expands beyond helping them. They want to feel comfortable, welcomed, and able to leisurely or quickly enjoy their shopping experience without the pressure of the salesperson watching them at every step. These same customers know that there are countless places they could choose to spend their money, so one wrong move in the store could leave enough of a bad taste that they choose to leave. If and when you decide to greet the customer, please keep the following in mind:

- **Make eye contact:** This creates a connection and assures you they have seen you as well.
- **Have friendly body language:** You should avoid slouching, turning your back to customers and approaching customers from behind. No one wants to be startled!
- **Take your time:** Don't immediately feel like you need to say hello when someone walks into your store. They should be in your store, not just walking through your door, before you say hello.

Consider what you will say, as well as what you won't say, once your customers are in your store. Simply saying "hello" is often the only thing you need to immediately say. Beyond this you should offer an additional greeting that lends itself to getting to know your customer more but, again, take your time.

Managers and salespeople should give the customer a chance to come in and browse the store before they start any conversation. A good practice is to watch the customer from afar to gather ideas about what they might be in for. Why engage the customer in a scripted conversation when we do not know what they are in for? The scripted conversation could turn out to be totally irrelevant to the customer's needs. The old saying: "whoever talks first loses" is totally true. Let the customer talk first so that you can understand what they want. If the customer wants something or wants information, they WILL ask you. What is the point of giving them a long-scripted speech only to find out that they are in just to take a look, or they are in to talk to customer service or to pick up something and leave?

Another good practice is to walk around the store not too far from the customer and occasionally make simple quick eye contact with them. This will show the customer that the salesperson is available to them in case they have a question but at the same time is not there to bother them.

In this guide for managers and salespeople the focus is on the fact that while companies teach their salespeople uniform structured sales approaches that have step by step scripted speeches, the real situation with every customer is unique and different. The salesperson must be able to adapt to each real situation with each customer. The salesperson must be dynamic and quick. Having said that, what is the point then of emphasizing a step-by-step approach when in reality the customer is the one who is going to dictate how the conversation is going to progress? As we will see in the upcoming chapters, the salesperson must just be a human being and must be armed with knowledge not with scripted obsolete step by step sales techniques that the customer is going to see through which will result in both parties feeling awkward.

Chapter Three: The Conversation.

From knowing which area of the store the customer is concentrating on to knowing who the customer came in with (friend or spouse) to watching their body language to overhearing their comments and conversations about the product whether it is very beautiful or very expensive or too small to having had a brief conversation with the customer already, the salesperson has many weapons in his/her arsenal to fight for the sale.

As previously mentioned, when the customers walk into a store, they do not want to see a salesperson; they want to see a human being who is knowledgeable about the product who is going to answer their questions using simple terms away from any specific industry jargon.

In chapter one we established that you do not look like a salesperson. In chapter two we established that you do not behave like a salesperson. Now we are going to establish that you will not be talking like a salesperson.

At whatever point in time during the customer's presence in the store, you should let the customer talk first. They will tell you what it is they are thinking about. Let's assume that you saw your customer hovering around a specific mattress. What is the point of starting the conversation with the customer about how great the mattress is and the fact that it is on sale only to find out that the customer already has the mattress, but they hate it and they are here for a new one as long as it is not the same one? Because of that both you and the customer now feel awkward. Instead, you should have let the customer tell you what was on their mind so you can proceed with a new mattress for them, one that has different features and perhaps more expensive. Now you are being an expert who is going to offer a solution instead of being an awkward salesperson. Do not be afraid to say it; tell the customer that you will offer them **a solution**. They will love you if you say that.

As mentioned, have a regular conversation with the customer. Speak in layperson terms. Stay away from any industry jargon because if you use industry jargon they will not understand, and maybe they did not care to know anyway, and you will run the risk of making your customer feel inferior. If the customer feels inferior, they will not be comfortable so they will not be buying.

Instead, know enough about the product to tell the customer the features and how these features will be beneficial to them. Now the customer looks up to you and they like you and if they like you, they will buy from you. As part of the conversation with the customer do not be afraid to be yourself; tell them about any personal experience with the product; tell them that another product is better but may be on sale; tell them any customer reviews about the product.

Listening to the customer is crucial. As a general rule, you should listen more than you talk even if you are a salesperson in the middle of the sale. The reason is that if you listen to your customer and read between the lines you will pick up so much information that will save you time and talk and will help you cut through to the right product and close the sale. On the other hand, if you listen carefully to the customer you will be able to determine if you need to spend time on trying to upsell or add warranties. Managers should stop telling their salespeople to try to upsell and get warranties on every sale (but that does not mean that the salesperson cannot be aggressive; the salesperson must be aggressive and will show you how later). Let's assume that the customer told the salesperson that they are looking for a mattress that is on sale for $399. Also, the customer told you as part of the conversation that they have been **saving to buy** the mattress and now that it went on sale for the right price, they are here to buy it. Who in the right mind would attempt to upsell the customer to a $2000 mattress? I know that your manager would tell you to try to upsell because you never know if the customer would like to finance the $2000 mattress. The answer is **NO**; just close it quickly and move on to the next customer without wasting anymore time. There are situations where you will sell a $2000 mattress to a customer who thought that they came in to buy a $399 mattress. For example, if that customer told you that they saw the $399 mattress advertised so they came in to check it out because they are trying to replace their old mattress, then for sure that customer just opened up a huge opportunity for you to let them walk away with ten times the amount they came in to spend. In this case you use reverse psychology which will be explained shortly.

Always listen to key words from your customers that will help you save time, make more money, and better serve the customer.   You will run into countless different situations. Let me give you some examples:

- "I am here to replace the stove for my **rental unit**". The customer wants a cheap stove.
- "**Customer service** said we can come in to select a new fridge because the **technician could not fix** the one we bought". Not only this is a sale, but also the customer will buy a better-quality fridge and they will buy the extended warranty with it.
- "We would like to buy a cheap mattress for the **guest room**".   You can suggest that the customer put the one they have in the guest room and buy a very nice new mattress for themselves.

Always have a simple conversation with the customer. Never include any key or scripted words because the customer will always see through them and when this happens you lose their trust.   Instead use Reverse Psychology!

What is reverse psychology when it comes to selling in a retail environment?   It is the simple science of excitement reversed by logic.   I have used reverse psychology for many years and the results were always amazing.   Let me illustrate with an example.   A customer comes in to buy a car. After you qualify the customer as applicable you demonstrate and promote the more expensive car. The customer will test drive it and because of its features and benefits the customer falls in love with it; people do like good things. Then you show the customer the cheaper car and let them drive it. Obviously the customer will not like it at all. Now you try to convince the customer that since both cars are similar why pay for the much more expensive one! However, by this time the customer is hooked to the more expensive car. As a rule, you always start with the best product no matter what that product is, then you try to convince the customer not to buy it while constantly reminding them of the features and benefits of that product. The result: they have developed an emotional attachment to the first product. On the other hand, you got the customer to believe that you are trustworthy because you are advising them not to buy the expensive product and you have paved the way to sell the customer any warranties or any add-ons that will double your income from that sale.

Reverse psychology can always be applied. Think of it as your alternative to being desperate. For example, you are desperate to sell a warranty, but you cannot show the customer that you are desperate. Instead, you ask the customer if they would like to learn about the warranty and you tell them that the warranty is completely optional and may be completely unnecessary for the product they are buying. Now they believe that you really do not care if you sell it or not, so they ask you to explain it. Now it is up to you to shine; if you explain it well, they will buy it because you showed them that you don't care if they do or not. As explained earlier your knowledge about the warranty is much better to have than an obsolete scripted step by step approach.

Reverse psychology can also be used in quick simple situations. For example, you may spot a customer in the store looking at a sofa. It was advertised that sofas are 30% off. All you have to do is walk by and tell the customer any other attribute about the sofa (how many colours it comes in, sizes, stock availability, etc.) and then walk away without looking back. If this customer ends up buying, then the sale will be yours because they will come back to you. This is much better than staying with the customer uninvited and doing a scripted speech.

One more piece of advice before we close the sale. Be calm and normal; no need to be overly happy and no need to use flashy words like fantastic, beautiful, fabulous, awesome, or delighted. Customers see through everything and they notice everything; no need to give them a chance to see that you are very happy you are getting the sale.

By now you do not look like a salesperson, you do not behave like a salesperson, and you do not talk like a salesperson. Let's see if we can close the sale seamlessly and with minimal effort next.

Chapter Four: Close The Sale, No Matter What.

In all the literature and the sales training courses there is a whole section about closing the sale. In all of these courses they tell you to "ask for the sale". Here, I am NOT going to ask the customer for the sale. Please do not ask the customer for the sale. The sale is assumed. It is implied. We all agree that when the customer is comfortable, when the salesperson is knowledgeable, when the salesperson is trustworthy, when the customer likes the salesperson, when the customer does not believe that the salesperson is trying to sell them something they do not want, and when the salesperson is not actually being a salesperson then the customer will buy and they will pay a premium price.

However, the customer may genuinely want to think about the purchase and not pull the trigger right away. In this case you have to overcome any possible objection by the customer to clear the way to write the sale on the spot and without any delay.

The traditional training courses have whole sections about overcoming customer objections. But we will continue to stay away from any scripted material. Remember it is still you, that salesperson who does not look like, behave like, or talk like a salesperson.

The most common customer objection is the price. In this case you need to ask one or both of these simple questions: "how far apart are we?", and "what can I do to earn your business today?". In the traditional literature they tell you that the customer objects to the price because the salesperson did not explain and demonstrate the quality, the features, and the benefits of the product. I am here to tell you that no matter how perfectly you explain the product the customer may still object to the price, so no need to waste time and just cut through to the end.

The sales managers need to empower their salespeople to make instant decisions without going back to the office. As a sales manager, it's clear that you work for the sales team instead of the team working for you. However, one of the biggest traps to avoid is to not let yourself be drawn into being nothing but a secretary for the sales team. And it's easy to get drawn in.

As far as you can according to company policies, provide your salespeople with not only the responsibility but also the ability to make decisions up to a certain point.   Whether it's pricing, terms, or other considerations, there is no way you can make every decision needed to operate a successful sales team. If you could, you wouldn't really need all those salespeople.

One of your first orders of business is to provide your sales team with tools, resources, and competitor data needed to make decisions. With these, the salesperson is able to close the price gap with the customer; again, actual price, terms, financing, and fees all fall under price. If price fails, your next line of attack is to try to secure a deposit on the sale. This is very powerful as you are effectively securing the commitment from the customer to come back. When they come back, they will pay in full or they will decide to cancel the order. If they decide to cancel, then most of the time a small tweak in the price or the terms will produce a final deal.

The third line of attack is to produce a sales quote based on the discounted price. The quote is also very powerful. It gives the customer a chance to think about the purchase and it will remind the customer that you invested time and effort and professionalism vis-a-vis the competition to earn the sale. More times than not the customer will come back to you to pay and close the deal perhaps, again, with a minor price tweak just to make the customer feel good that they decided to come back.

When it comes to selling warranties and add-ons, as we discussed earlier, use reverse psychology most of the time. Warranties and add-ons usually pay you much higher income than the regular product, so it is in your best interest to sell them. Make sure that the warranty and add-on are presented to the customer whenever possible and throughout the sale. In case the customer refuses the warranty, it is important not to give up. For example, let us assume that the selling price of a sofa is $2500 and the warranty on it is $309. You presented the benefits of the warranty and you used the reverse psychology tactic but still the customer does not want it. Your next line of attack is to let the customer know that from your experience you cannot leave this sofa unprotected so what you are willing to do for them is give them an extra discount on the sofa in order to fit the warranty in. There are many formulas that you can use but the most common is to give them an extra $150 off the sofa so you can add the warranty for $309. In this case the total price that the customer would pay is $2659, not $2809. From my experience about 95% of the customers welcome this arrangement. The other 5% require an additional discount for this arrangement and your job is to accommodate all 100% of the customers. As mentioned above there are countless cases and scenarios, and each is as unique as each customer. We must accommodate each customer and work with them in order to create a win-win situation each and every time. Do not be afraid to negotiate with the customer and do not be afraid to tell them that the goal is to arrive at a win-win situation such that they will save money because they are buying from you, and you will make the most money from the sale. This is when we see the enormous value of empowerment by the sales manager. The salespeople should be able to make these win-win situation decisions without going back to the sales manager for approval. The result will be efficient and effective salespeople who will move on to the next customer quicker, more respectful and happier customers because that salesperson looked to them like he or she was the one who made the decision to give an extra discount to close the deal, dedicating managers who now have more time to do more important things for the store and the salespeople, and more sales for the company and more income for the salesperson thus less attrition and turnover.

What is the point of giving up on the warranty when in the worst case scenario you can add it with a small discount on the merchandise? So, by now you do not close deals like a salesperson.

One of the biggest misconceptions in the sales industry is that closing the deal is the end of the initial sales process. It is an important step, but it is not a one-time event. Good salespeople know how to close a deal, but they stop selling after implementing their solution. However, great salespeople not only know how to close the deal, but they continue to add value to their clients, build repeat business, and create referrals.

In the sales training courses, they always talk about the 80/20 rule; only 20% of the customers buy but if you are a great salesperson you close some of the remaining 80%. As a non-traditional salesperson my 80/20 rule is that 80% of salespeople report giving up on a customer after hearing "no" three times, and 80% of customers report saying "no" three times before they finally say "yes". So please stick with those 80% of the customers and do not give up on them.

Always remember that there is a reason that made a customer come to the store. There is a reason that they are here today. The customers know that there are plenty of similar stores selling the same or similar products. What is it that will make them buy from you TODAY? Once you find out you MUST grant them that thing. That thing may be price, it may be their experience at your store, or it may be a combination of many things. Never let the customer walk away without buying if you can create a win-win situation. We all know that customers will find the same car for example in every showroom. The customer is at your store after visiting other stores only to find out that the car is the same price across all stores. The sales manager will immediately think that he/she should be firm on the price because the customer will not find a better price, so he/she is willing to let them walk away without buying. It is a crime to do that. The customer is at your store and the product and the price are identical across all stores. Thus, the sales manager and the salesperson must immediately find a reason outside these two factors to close that customer. It could be a free mug, free delivery, free upgrade, a gift from the manufacturer, a gift card for future purchase, or stock availability. If none of these can be offered, you must differentiate on price to close the customer immediately. Finally, always remember that a smaller commission is better than no commission at all and it is better than a full commission that may come later tonight or tomorrow.

Another line of attack to close the sale is the second face. As the name implies, if for whatever reason you are very close to closing the deal, but you are unable to, you should bring in a second face. The second face could be your sales manager or one of the more experienced colleagues. The role of the second face can be one or more of the following. The second face will act as **the expert** in the eyes of the customer. The second face is to assure the customer and reinforce the fact that the deal they got is great and sensible. The second face will review the order and remind the customer of any warranties or add-ons as applicable. The second face will tell the customer based on real life stories how the product fits their needs and how much more money they could have paid under the normal circumstances. The second face will give examples about why the customer is better off with the more expensive product and about how, based on real stories from past customers, the warranty or add-on is so worth it to them in terms of protection or extra savings. Please remember that the sales process is dynamic, not a static step by step, so you can ask the second face to get engaged in the conversation any time or multiple times during the customer's presence in the store.

It would be wonderful if you choose the second face based on the propensity of the customer being able to relate to the second face. For example, if the customer is a female, bring in a female. If the customer is black, bring in a black second face. If the customer is Indian or Chinese, bring in an Indian or a Chinese second face so that the second face can speak with the customer using the same language. This could be so powerful and beneficial not only for closing this sale but also for having this customer as a repeat customer who can even bring in referrals.

On the other hand, the second face is so powerful when for whatever reason the customer does not like you. For example, a female customer is hoping to talk to a female salesperson because she wants a woman's opinion. A black customer can see a black salesperson in the store and the customer wants to talk to a black salesperson. A Chinese customer would rather speak with a Chinese salesperson. There is ABSOLUTELY nothing wrong with any of the above. If you bring in a second face the customer will appreciate you and they will respect you and you can assume that they will buy today. Next time you can return the favour to that second face when they need a second face.

Chapter Five: Eliminating Remorse, And A Second Face To Reinforce.

Buyer's remorse is common and cannot be overlooked by a successful salesperson. Contrary to traditional beliefs eliminating buyer's remorse is actually a process that starts with the conversation with the customer. During the conversation with the customer, you had to explain the features and benefits of the product, you had to talk about the warranty and its benefits, and you had to talk about any financing options that will make it so much easier for the customer to buy. All of the above eliminate buyer's remorse. *The only thing that you have to keep in mind is the fact that all of the above **actually** eliminate buyer's remorse!* Meaning if you are conscious of that then your words, your enthusiasm, and your body language will be more effective and are the building blocks for the customer's confidence about the purchase. Traditionally, the step-by-step sales techniques emphasize eliminating buyer's remorse at the end of the sale. I have seen some training courses that do not even mention buyer's remorse at all or hide buyer's remorse under what they call Follow Up. Those courses would have a big section about following up with the customer to thank them for their purchase. We will talk about that later.

So the process of eliminating remorse continues to the end of the sale. This is when the magic of reverse psychology comes into play. I usually be as frank as I can be and tell customers that they can actually cancel the order. When they feel comfortable about the fact that they have the power to cancel the order, they will not. I usually tell my customers the following (you can choose your words based on your personality): *"the most important thing is to be happy and comfortable with your purchase. I know that when the customer leaves the store, they cannot wait to get home to tell family and friends about what they bought and how happy they are with it only to be faced with criticism. I know that family or friends may tell you that you are crazy to spend that much. They will say that you should have waited because 2 months ago it was on sale for much cheaper or whatever they may tell you. If that happens please call me and I will cancel the order right away because like I said I want you to be comfortable".* When the customer actually goes home and is actually faced with a variety of ideas and criticisms about their purchase that would lead to order cancellation, they would be psychologically immune to those ideas and criticisms because what you told the customer would happen at home actually happened. Being psychologically immune means that the customer would feel that you and them are on the same team against family and friends, and not the customer and family on the same team against you.

Yet another weapon to eliminate remorse is the second face. As we discussed earlier, the second face helped with closing the deal (even though you may have gotten them engaged much earlier). When the second face was helping you close the deal, he/she was actually eliminating remorse as well. We discussed that the second face acts as the expert in the eyes of the customer. We said the role of the second face is to assure the customer and reinforce the fact that the deal they got is great and sensible. We said that the second face will review the order and remind the customer of any warranties or add-ons as applicable. We said the second face will tell the customer based on real life stories how the product fits their needs and how much more money they could have paid under normal circumstances. And we said the second face will give examples about why the customer is better off with the more expensive product and about how the warranty or add-on is so worth it to them in terms of protection or extra savings. All of these will help eliminate buyers' remorse.

Finally, we discussed that it would be wise if you choose the second face based on the propensity of the customer being able to relate to the second face. If the customer is a female, bring in a female. If the customer is black, bring in a black second face. If the customer is Indian or Chinese, bring in a second face that is Indian or Chinese. If the customer can relate to the second face, then the chance of remorse being eliminated is much higher.

So, we can see that eliminating remorse is a process, not a step with a scripted speech. Once you actually think of eliminating remorse as a process you will be so good at it and it will come as second nature thus you and the customer are comfortable under any scenario.

Once you have done what you can to eliminate remorse then there would be no need to call the customer to follow up to make sure they are happy with the purchase and answer any questions and thank them for doing business with you. In fact, it would be redundant to call the customer; if the customer needs something they will call you for sure. All of the traditional sales training courses would tell you to call the customer after the sale, but I am here to tell you that you do not need to call the customer. Even if you do not bring in a second face may be because you feel confident about the deal, or if a second face is not available please do not call the customer after the sale. Your manager will tell you that following up with your customer will generate referrals for you. I am telling you that because of the way you handled yourself throughout the sale so far you will never be forgotten by your customer. How could your customer forget a non-traditional salesperson like you?

I never call my customers after the sale. Once I tried an experiment by actually calling the customer the next day to thank them for their purchase and to see if they have any questions. I will never forget what happened: the couple started asking all kinds of questions and they talked about the price and they talked about finding other models on the website. They ended up coming back to the store to reselect their products and cancelled the warranty. What if I never called them? Would they have called me? We will never find out. Just do a good job while the customer is there and never call them after they leave. If they need you, they will call you.

Conclusions.

You are now liberated, and so is your customer. You are now a regular human being who has the oldest profession in history as a career, not just a job. You no longer look odd in your non-fitting suit and tie. You look comfortable and happy. You are no longer a robot reciting scripted sentences to the customer. The customer is a human being, and they deserve likewise to talk to. You are smart, quick, honest, and frank and you are making a lot of money.

I never said that well invested well-dressed salespeople are bad or not successful. They are great but the vast majority for sure would be better off dressing down. One objective takeaway from this guide is to let salespeople look great whether they choose to dress up or dress down.

Another takeaway is the fact that the conversation with the customer, the greeting of the customer, and the close of the deal are processes NOT chronological steps. In countless times I greet the customer way after we have started talking about the product and way after

I started answering questions; I just say: "by the way my name is Mo". There is absolutely nothing wrong with that.

Reverse psychology is truly a wonderful thing. It is a tool that can certainly make you a lot of money. Albeit rare, I have had savvy customers who saw through what I was doing and told me that they have never had a salesperson like me. Despite the fact that these rare customers knew exactly what I was doing they still went for the expensive product and the warranty.

Enough talking about the weather and how cute the baby is. Be direct, firm, and up to the point. Stop using fillers to start a conversation or in a conversation with the customer. Be respectful and happy and be unorthodox. Your customers are going to be delighted.